CONTENTS

PREFACE 1
A LIST OF WORKS USED. 10
BEN SIRA'S PROVERBS PRESERVED IN TALMUDIC 14
AND RABBINIC LITERATURE.

PREFACE

IN editing the recently discovered Hebrew fragments of the book of Ben Sira, we have limited our aim to presenting the original text with as little delay as possible, and at the same time giving in a convenient form the materials for further study. A full commentary, as well as a detailed comparison of the versions, must be left for the future. We shall therefore not discuss the author's full name, or the date of his composition or of the Greek and Syriac translations[1]. For the literature on these points the reader is referred to Schürer's admirable work on 'The History of the Jewish People in the time of Jesus Christ[2].' In what follows we shall confine ourselves to some remarks on what is known, from Jewish sources, of Ben Sira and his writings.

It is now generally admitted that Jesus, son of Sirach (Σειράχ, סירא [3]) of Jerusalem, wrote his ethical work (usually quoted as 'the book of Ben Sira [4]'), in Hebrew, between 200 and 170 B. C. in Jerusalem. It was translated into Greek by his grandson, as stated in the prologue, from which we also gather that the version was made from the Hebrew, in the year 132 B. C. [5] The Hebrew of the present fragment is (with the exceptions referred to below, p. XIII) *classical*, not Rabbinical: still less is it an Aramaic dialect, such as that of several of the passages quoted in both Talmuds (the Palestinian [6] as well as the Babylonian), in the Midrashim, and in later Hebrew writings.

In early times the book seems to have hovered on the verge of the canon, or to have been included among the כתובים (Hagiographa, see p. XXII below), since quotations from it are introduced by שנאמר (*as it is said*), a phrase applied only to the sacred writings. Although afterwards excluded from the canon by the Rabbis, it continued to live and to be appreciated both in the Palestinian and the Babylonian schools, as is proved by the fact that the text was constantly quoted either in the original or in a Rabbinical or Aramaic form. The Rabbis who lived before the destruction of the Temple used it without acknowledgement in the 'Sentences of the Fathers' (פרקי אבות, the earliest production of Rabbinical literature), while others quote from it either expressly under the name of Ben Sira, or anonymously, or else base their maxims upon it [7]. Rabbi Akiba and Ben Azai borrowed from it *verbatim* [8], and there is reason to believe that some apocryphal books were influenced by it [9]. Thus the official exclusion from the canon did not involve destruction, as in the case of some Christian uncanonical Gospels and Acts: the book of Sirach was allowed to be freely read, but it was regarded merely as literature and not as sacred [10]. Passing on to the later history of the book, we find that S. Jerome [11] (fourth century A. D.) possessed a Hebrew copy, although he did not translate it. That the book continued to be known, to individuals at least if not generally, is proved by the passages quoted from it (in a language already debased), by the Rabbis of the fifth and sixth centuries, in the later Midrashim of the seventh and eighth centuries (as the Tanḥuma), and in the sayings collected by R. Nathan in the ninth century [12]. Zunz (op. cit., p. 108, end of note e) believes that the early liturgist, R. Eleazar haq-Qalir, borrowed from Sirach (l. 5-8) in his liturgy for the day of Atonement, in praise of the High Priest. Simultaneously some of the sayings of Sirach are quoted by the Babylonian doctors in an Aramaic form [13].

For the tenth century we are on even firmer ground as to the existence of the book in its original language. R. Seadyah (סעדיה) Gaon, of Bagdad (920 A. D.), and of the Fayyum in Egypt, was blamed by the Qaraites [14] for sending out missives written in Hebrew provided with vowel-points and accents. They reproached him with endeavouring to give to his correspondence an appearance of holiness equal to that of the Biblical text, since the vowel-points and accents were supposed, according to tradition, to have been given with the Law on Mount Sinai. In answer to this accusation Seadyah [15] states that these additions to the text are found also in copies of Ben Sira, in the book of the Wisdom of Eleazar ben Irai (Iri [16]), and in the scroll of the Hasmoneans [17]. In the course of his defence he quotes seven (or rather eight, see note 2 below) genuine sayings of Sirach in classical Hebrew, so that it may be concluded that the book was at his disposal in the tenth century. The mentions of Ben Sira after this date are scanty and uncertain. R. Nissim ben Jacob (eleventh century) of Kairowân, in Tunisia, makes a quotation, which however he may have derived from S^eadyah. In the eleventh century, according to Reifmann [18], signs of Sirach's influence appear in the collection of sayings entitled מבחר הפנינים (Choice of Pearls), attributed to the famous poet and philosopher Solomon ben Gabirol [19] (Avicebron). The same scholar [20] also finds traces of the influence of Sirach (II. 18) in the Jewish daily prayer [21], and (XLIX. 10 and 11) in the hymn [22] for the outgoing of the Sabbath. He contends further that Sirach has an allusion (I. 2) to Aristotle and the doctrine of the eternity of matter, and that even Spinoza was perhaps influenced by Sirach (XLIV. 34). These suggestions, as well as the inference (from the Aramaic form of the proverb, No. LIV below), that he was an Essene, are, to say the least, not convincing. There is no direct trace of the existence of the Hebrew Sirach in Spain, Provence, or among the Rabbis of France, the Rhine-land, and Germany. Rashi, the authors of the glosses on the Talmud (תוספות), and even Maimonides [23], did not possess the book; and later Rabbis, who mention sentences from it, most probably quoted second-hand from older authorities [24]. No doubt it might be said, though the supposition is not very probable, that all the quotations from Sirach were made from memory, and that they were derived from oral tradition. Recent discoveries however have removed all uncertainty on this point.

Mrs. Lewis, who brought to light the now famous codex of the Syriac Gospels in the convent on Mount Sinai, some time ago acquired some manuscript fragments in the East [25], among which Mr. S. Schechter, Reader in Talmudic in the University of Cambridge, recognized one leaf as containing a fragment of Sirach (XXXIX. 15 to XL. 7) in Hebrew, which he published with English translation, introduction, and notes in the *Expositor* for July 1896, (p. I seqq.). Through the kindness of the owner we have since been allowed to make a fresh examination of the leaf, and have found reason to alter some of the readings accepted by Mr. Schechter (see the Hebrew text, pp. 2 and 4).

Although the leaf is mutilated in places, the parts which are still intact are abundantly sufficient to show the character and style of the composition, and to convince critics that the text is original and not a translation. After pointing this out, Mr. Schechter rightly adds: 'Its correspondence with the versions changes almost in every line, agreeing in some places with the Greek, in others with the Syriac. In other places, again, it agrees with *neither* of these versions, omitting whole clauses which are to be found both in the Greek and in the Syriac, or offering new readings which have been either misunderstood or misread by the translators. Certain clauses, again, are to be found in our MS. which are wanting in *both* versions, or are only reproduced by a very short paraphrase. There cannot, therefore, be even the shadow of a doubt that our text represents nothing else but the original. Even the marginal glosses testify to this fact. Such differences of *plena* and *defectiva* as צורך and צרך, or such fine variants as פיו and פיהו, cannot possibly have been suggested by any translation, and could only have been made from some other copy of the original.'

Almost simultaneously the Bodleian Library acquired, through Professor Sayce, a box of Hebrew and Arabic fragments, among which we recognized another portion of the same text of Sirach, consisting of nine leaves, and forming the continuation of Mrs. Lewis' leaf, from chapter XL. 9 to XLIX. 11. These fragments cannot be part of the copy mentioned by S^eadyah, since they are not provided with vowel-points or accents, and also because the writing is not of the tenth century, but of the end of the eleventh [26] at the earliest, as may be seen from the facsimiles. The MS. does not seem to us to have been written by a Qaraite. There are in both fragments marginal notes [27] giving the variants of another copy of Sirach, or more probably of two other copies. These copies were however incomplete, the marginal notes giving their variants only as far as chapter XLV. 8 (see note in loco), and on XLVII. 8 and 9. In the Bodleian fragment there are also at least two Persian glosses (ff. 1 and 5^b), which point to its having been written in Bagdad or Persia, possibly transcribed from S^eadyah's copy. The MS. is written on oriental paper, and is arranged in lines, eighteen to the page (in Mrs. Lewis' leaf one line is cut off), and the lines are divided into hemistichs. There is no indication of chapters, but a line is left blank occasionally, as shown in our printed text. The MS. is unfortunately damaged in many places, which we have marked by clots, showing approximately the number of letters missing, and by [ ] when letters are supplied. Our object being however to give the text of Sirach as we found it, we have carefully restricted conjecture to its narrowest limits. In some cases we have preferred to leave a lacuna, where either the space in the MS. did not allow of what seemed the obvious word, or some letter such as ל, ז, or ק was excluded; see e. g. xlv. 13^b. In every case a letter about which we felt there could be any reasonable doubt, has been marked with a horizontal stroke, thus א̄. On some orthographical peculiarities of the MS. see the note appended to the glossary, p. XXXVI. As regards the translation again, we have deemed it our duty as editors of a unique manuscript, to express the text faithfully, and not to adopt conjectural readings, except where the text yielded absolutely no sense. Usually, indeed, the meaning is clear; but passages occur which, from whatever cause, are obscure, and we cannot feel confident that we have seized the sense of all of them. A (?) in the translation indicates doubt either as to the reading or the rendering. There are sufficient indications that the text is not. everywhere in its original purity, and we do not doubt that (as in many parts of the O. T.) cases will be found in which a purer reading has been preserved by one or other of the early versions; but a detailed comparison of the Hebrew text and the versions, and a discussion of their comparative merits, must, we think, be left to a commentary, as well as to a time when, we may hope, more of the original shall have been recovered. We have noted, lastly, the more important places in which the language is coloured by reminiscences of the Old Testament.

The language, as already observed, is classical Hebrew, the syntax displaying no traces of the peculiar New-Hebrew constructions, such as occur, for instance, so frequently in Ecclesiastes [28], though the vocabulary has an admixture of late or Aramaic words or expressions, such as might be expected from the date at which the author wrote. The latter, together with other words not occurring in Biblical Hebrew, will be found collected in the glossary (p. XXXI). The style is occasionally a little heavy, but this may sometimes be due to corruption of the text. Otherwise (especially chap. XLIV. ff.) it is remarkably easy and flowing. It stands throughout on an altogether higher level than that, for instance, of Chronicles, Ecclesiastes, or the Hebrew parts of Daniel. We know from Ecclesiastes that the New-Hebrew idiom was in process of formation at this time, and it is evident that both New-Hebrew and

Aramaic [29] words were current in the Hebrew with which the author was familiar; but the predominant character of his style is nevertheless pure and classical. The marginal readings are often interesting: the variations which they indicate are frequently considerably greater than those noted by the Massorites in the O. T., and resemble rather the various readings often presupposed by the LXX, while at other times they are noticeable as giving an Aramaic equivalent for a Hebrew word in the text. Sirach's position with regard to the New-Hebrew would no doubt be made clearer by the discovery of the originals of other apocryphal books, such as Judith, Maccabees i, Enoch, and the Psalms of Solomon. Finally the theory that he wrote his proverbs in metre is not supported by the newly-recovered text: the lines are very variable in length, and there is no indication that the author sought to adapt them to a uniform metrical scheme.

In the present edition we give:

- (*a*) The Hebrew text, with the marginal notes and glosses arranged as in the MS.
- (*b*) The English translation of the Hebrew, adopting as far as possible the diction of the revised version of the O. T.
- (*c*) The Syriac version (which was made from the Hebrew), according to Lagarde's edition, a blank space indicating that the translator, or copyist, omitted a passage
- (*d*) The Greek translation, according to Dr. Swete's edition, the blanks again indicating such omissions. The uncertain condition of the Greek text is well illustrated by Hatch [30], and will strike the reader on even a slight examination. Its value for comparative purposes is further lessened by the translator's tendency to paraphrase, as is the case also with the Syriac.
- (*e*) At the end, the Old Latin, according to Lagarde's edition of the Codex Amiatinus. For more convenient reference we have in all five texts numbered the chapters and verses as in Dr. Swete's edition, and indicated the hemistichs by letters of the alphabet in order. The Syriac, Greek, and Latin texts are reproduced exactly as in the editions followed. It did not fall within our plan to give the variants of these versions.
- (*f*) A glossary of noticeable words and expressions.

- (*g*) A list of proverbs attributed to Sirach in Talmudic and Rabbinical literature, with a translation, arranged in the order of the Greek version. Here again we resolved not to add the various readings, since the Talmudic dialect is not the original language of Sirach, and moreover, all the new Talmudic fragments found within the last two years have not yet been collated.

For completeness sake we have added the so-called 'Alphabets' of Ben Sira, a late composition--probably of the eleventh century or perhaps even later, but containing some genuine proverbs of Sirach, both in the first and second parts [31]. The stories given after each proverb in part I. are mostly indecent, and written in mockery of Jewish literature. We reproduce the first אב (MS. second), with a translation: for the second (MS. first), we only refer to the numbers in our list of proverbs with which it agrees, ignoring the rest as alien to Sirach. The Alphabets [32], though a late and unedifying compilation [33], survived, whilst Ecclesiasticus was completely neglected. A Persian text of them was lately acquired by the British Museum (MS. Or. 4731), and another copy has just been brought by Mr. E. N. Adler from Persia, probably translated from the Constantinople edition (see below, p. XXIX). (*h*) Some specimens of attempted restorations of the original Hebrew by modern scholars confronted with our text. The comparison will, we think, justify the caution and reservation which must be observed in attempting to restore lost works on the basis of ancient translations [34]. In the present instance, for example, both versions prove to be much freer than was assumed to be the case by those who so used them.

In conclusion, we have great pleasure in acknowledging the help of friends who have enabled us to carry through the work in a short time in spite of difficulties. Mr. J. F. Stenning, of Wadham College, rendered valuable aid in deciphering the difficult parts of the MS., including the Cambridge leaf, and in all doubtful places he concurs in the readings which we have adopted in our text. He also revised the Syriac. Mr. E. N. Bennett, of Hertford College, read the Greek: Rev. F. E. Brightman, Librarian of the Pusey House, read the Latin. Professor D. S. Margoliouth has also shown an interest in the work in various ways. We feel, however, specially grateful to the Regius Professor of Hebrew, Dr.

Driver. He revised the translation throughout, besides being entirely responsible for the glossary, with the note appended, and almost every page of the book owes something to the judgement and accuracy which he has been always ready to expend upon it.

---

1. On this subject, see E. Hatch, *Essays in Biblical Greek*, VII. p. 254 seq.
2. English translation, 2nd division, vol. III. p. 23 seqq. (Clark, Edinburgh, 1886); and later, his article on 'Apocryphen des Alten Testaments' in the *Realencyclopädie für protestantische Theologie und Kirche*, vol. I. p. 650 seqq. (3rd ed., Leipzig, 1896).
3. Schürer, op. cit., p. 25, explains the name to mean 'coat of mail.' In the Hebrew Josippon (Pseudo-Josephus) the form שירך is a transliteration from the Latin; v. Zunz, *Die gottesdienstlichen Vorträge der Juden*, 2nd ed., 3892, p. 107, note *h*. He was not, as sometimes stated, a priest; Zunz, ibid., p. 106.
4. So most frequently in early Rabbinic literature. S. Jerome (see p. x, note 5) says that it was called *Parabolae* (משלים) in Hebrew; cf. Ecclus. l. 27, and the use of משל (p. xxvi) and מתלא (p. xx) in the quotations. According to Seadyah (ספר הגלוי, ed. Harkavy, p. 151, lines 11 and 32) Ben Sira wrote a book of instruction (, ספר מוסר? see our text, p. 10, l. 8) similar in character to the book of Proverbs.
5. The many passages in which the translator has misunderstood his original, written only some sixty years before his own time, may perhaps serve as a warning to those scholars who are inclined to overrate the authority of the LXX version of the Old Testament.
6. It is remarkable that only five quotations are found in the Palestinian Talmud; see below, p. xix seqq. (Nos. I. b, XVII, XXVI, XXXII, LIV).
7. The quotations were first collected by Asaria de Rossi. For a list of them, see below, pp. XIX to XXVIII, and, for the literature dealing with them, Zunz, op. cit., pp. 108, 109, and notes.
8. Bacher, *Die Agada der Tannaiten*, I. p. 277, note 2; p. 417, notes 1 and 2.
9. See e. g. the list of parallel passages cited by Mr. Charles in *The Book of the Secrets of Enoch* (Oxford, 1896), p. 96, Index I; and Ryle and James, *The Psalms of Solomon* (Cambridge, 1891), p. LXIII seq.
10. הקורא בהן כקורא באיגרת, J. T. Synhedrin x. 5.
11. The well-known passage in his preface to the translation of the books of Solomon is as follows: 'Fertur et πανάρετος Jesu filii Sirach liber et alius ψευδεπίγραφος, qui Sapientia Salomonis inscribitur. Quorum priorem Hebraicum repperi, non Ecclesiasticum ut apud Latinos, sed Parabolas praenotatum, cui juncti erant Ecclesiastes et Canticum Canticorum, ut similitudinem Salomonis non solum librorum numero, sed etiam materiarum genere coaequaret.' S. Jerome simply adopted the old Latin version of the book; see pp. XXXVII to XLVII.
12. Critically re-edited by S. Schechter, Vindobonae, 1887.
13. Dalman, *Grammatik*, p. 29.
14. A Jewish sect which sprang up in the eighth century under Anan (ענן), and denied the authority of oral tradition. See Harkavy in *Grätz Geschichte d. Juden*, 3rd ed., vol. v. p. 413 (note 17).
15. ספר הגלוי, p. 162.
16. עיראי or עירי. It is curious to note that the saying . . . במופלא ממך (p. xix), ascribed in the Talmud to Ben Sira and found in the Greek version, is quoted by Seadyah

(op. cit., p. 178, l. 18) as belonging to the Wisdom of Ben Irai. Of this Eleazar b. Irai, Seadyah also quotes two other sentences in classical Hebrew, but not in so easy a style as roost of Sirach. He says Ben Irai's book of Wisdom is analogous to Ecclesiastes, while Ben Sira resembles the book of Proverbs. Of this enigmatical Eleazar ben Irai nothing further is known. Perhaps he is identical with the R. Eleazar who often reports sayings בשם בן סירא (see p. xix). Bacher (*Die Agada d. Palästinischen Amoräer*, ii. 1896, p. II, note 5) identifies him, not very plausibly, with Eleazar ben Pedath.

17. Edited by Dr. M. Gaster; see Notice in *Jewish Quarterly Review*, VI. p. 570.
18. In the Hebrew periodical האסיף, III. p. 250.
19. See Steinschneider, *Die Hebräischen Uebersetzungen*, p. 382 seqq. (§S 225).
20. In the essay on Ben Sira in his ארבעה חרשים (Prag, 1860), p. 3 seqq.
21. See the Authorised Daily Prayer Book, with a new translation by the Rev. S. Singer, p. 62, נפלה נא ביד יהוה כי רבים רחמיו וגו׳.
22. Beginning אליהו הנביא. It is not included in the English Authorised Daily Prayer Book.
23. The Sira he quotes in his Commentary on the Mishna (Sanh. XI. I) must he, to judge from his low opinion of him, the compiler of the Alphabet; cf. Reifmann, האסיף, III. p. 251.
24. As e. g. Joseph ben Nahmias, *Jewish Quarterly Review*, IV. p. 164.
25. See *Jewish Quarterly Review*, IX. p. 115 seqq.
26. Mr. Schechter (ibid., p. 4) considers it 'certainly not later than the beginning of the twelfth century.'
27. These are indicated in the MS. by a small circle ° over the word in the text, which we reproduce.
28. The relative ש never occurs; the imperfect with ו consecutive occurs frequently; the perfect with ו consecutive in 42, 1c. 8c. 11c; the perfect with simple ו only in 39, 32. 44, 2. 16. 20b. 48, n. 12d.
29. The strong Syriasms which sometimes occur, deserve notice, as ממריו (42, 5c) and תסתויד (42) 12b).
30. Op. cit., p. 258 seqq.
31. In the Bodleian MS. No. 1466 the order is reversed.
32. The *Editio princeps* is that of Constantinople, 1519. (The Bodleian copy is defective.) For the other editions, see Steinschneider's *Catalogus Librorum Hebraeorum in Bibliotheca Bodleiana*, Berolini, 1852-1860; and Zedner's *Catalogue of Hebrew Books in the British Museum* (London, 1867), with Van Straalen's *Supplement* (1894).
33. See Reifmann, Hakarmel II. p. 124 seq.
34. Cf. Driver in *The Oxford Magazine*, vol. VIII (1890), no. 11, p. 182, and no. 12, p. 190 seq.

A LIST OF WORKS USED.

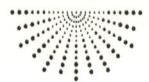

*B*ACHER (W.), Die Agada der babylonischen Amoräer. Strassburg, 1878.

------ Die Agada der Tannaiten. Strassburg, 1884.

BALL (C. J.), The Ecclesiastical or Deutero-Canonical Books of the Old Testament, commonly called the Apocrypha, edited with various renderings and readings from the best Authorities. [The Variorum Bible], Eyre and Spottiswoode, London, n. d.

BEN SEES (Wolfsohn, Jehuda Loeb), ... חכמת יהושע בן סירא נעתק בלשון עברי. Wien, 1814.

BICKELL (G.), Die Strophik des Ecclesiasticus, in the Vienna Oriental Journal, VI. (1892), p. 87. Compare his restoration of the alphabetical poem (51, 13-20) in the Zeitschrift für Katholische Theologie, 1882, p. 326 seqq.

CORONEL (N. N.), חמשה קונטרסים (for the Baraitha Kallah). Vindobonae, 1864.

DALMAN (G.), Grammatik des Jüdisch-Palästinischen Aramäisch. Leipzig, 1894.

DRIVER (S. R.) in the Oxford Magazine, vol. VIII. no. 11 (p. 182), and no. 12 (p. 190). Oxford, 1890.

DUKES (L.), Zur rabbinischen Spruchkunde. Wien, 1851.

------ Rabbinische Blumenlese. Leipzig, 1844.

EDERSHEIM (A.) in the Holy Bible . . . . . with an explanatory and critical commentary, &c. Apocrypha, edited by Henry Wace, D. D., vol. II. London (Murray), 1888.

EICHHORN, Bibliothek. Leipzig, 1787 &c. (vol. II. p. 691 seqq.).

FRANKEL (S. I.), כתובים אהרונים, Hagiographa posteriora . . . in linguam Hebraicam convertit . . . S. Isaac Fränkel. Lipsiae, 1830.

FRITZSCHE (O. F.), Libri Apocryphi Veteris Testamenti. Lipsiae, 1871.

GABIROL (R. Salomon ibn), ספר מבחר הפנינים, A Choice of Pearls, originally compiled from the Arabic ... translated into Hebrew by R. Jehuda ibn Tibbon, the Hebrew text ... accompanied by a faithful English translation by the Rev. B. H. Ascher. London (Trübner), 5619-1859.

GEIGER (A.) in the Zeitschrift der Deutschen Morgenländischen Gesellschaft, vol. XII. (p. 536 seqq.).

GRÄTZ (H.), Geschichte der Juden. Leipzig, 1874.

HAMBURGER (J.), Real-Encyclopädie für Bibel und Talmud. Supplement, Band I. p. 77 seqq. (art. Jesus Sohn Sirach). Leipzig, 1886.

HARKAVY (A.), Studien u. Mittheilungen aus der Kaiserlichen Oeffentlichen Bibliothek zu St. Petersburg: fünfter Theil, erstes Heft. St. Petersburg, 1891.

HATCH (E.), Essays in Biblical Greek (p. 246 seqq.). Oxford, 1889.

HOROWITZ (J.) in the Monatsschrift für Geschichte u. Wissenschaft des Judenthums, vol. XIV. (p. 1 of seqq., p. 136 seqq., p. 178 seqq.).

KOHUT (A.), Aruch completum. Viennae, 1878-1892.

LAGARDE (P. A. de), Libri Veteris Testamenti Apocryphi Syriace. Lipsiae, 1861.

------ Mittheilungen. Göttingen, 1884 (p. 285 seqq.).

LAMBERT (M.), Commentaire sur le Séfer Yesira . . . par le Gaon Saadya. Paris, 1891.

MARGOLIOUTH (D. S.) in the Expositor, April and May, 1890.

MIDRASH TANḤUMA, ed. Warsaw, 1879.

------ RABBA. Frankfurt, 1705.

NEUBAUER (Ad.) in the Jewish Quarterly Review, vol. IV. (p. 162 seqq.).

------ Catalogue of Hebrew MSS. in the Bodleian Library. Oxford, 1886.

RAPOPORT (S. J.) in the Hebrew periodical בסורי העתים, x. p. 116 seqq. (on Qalir). Wien, 1829.

REIFMANN (J.) in the periodical האסיף, vol. iii. Warsaw, 1886.

------ מאמר ארבעה חרשים. Prag, 1860.

------ in the periodical הכרמל, II. p. 124 seqq. Wilna, 1873.

DE Rossi (Asaria), מאור עינים, section אמרי בינה (p. 29 seqq.). Mantua, 1574.

SCHECHTER (S.) in the Jewish Quarterly Review, vol. III. no. 12 (July, 1891).

------ in the Expositor, 5th series, no. XIX. (July, 1896).

------ Aboth de Rabbi Nathan. Vindobonae, 1887.

SCHÜRER (E.) in the English translation, A History of the Jewish People in the time of Jesus Christ, 2nd division, vol. III. Edinburgh, 1886.

------ in the Realencyclopädie für protestantische Theologie und Kirche, 3rd ed. Leipzig, 1896 (art. Apocryphen des Alten Testaments).

Sᵉ ADYAH, ספר הגלוי, in, in Studien u. Mittheilungen aus der Kaiserlichen Oeffentlichen Bibliothek zu St. Petersburg, von Dr. A. Harkavy: fünfter Theil, erstes Heft. St. Petersburg, 1891.

SINGER (S.), The Authorised Daily Prayer Book. London, 5655-1895.

STEINSCHNEIDER (M.), אלפאביתא רבן סירא, Alphabetum Siracidis utrumque. Berolini, 1858.

------ Die Hebräischen Uebersetzungen des Mittelalters. Berlin, 1893.

------ Catalogus Librorum Hebraeorum in Bibliotheca Bodleiana. Berolini, 1852-1860.

STRAALEN (S. van), Catalogue of Hebrew Books in the British Museum. (London), 1894.

SWETE (H. B., D. D.), The Old Testament in Greek according to the LXX, vol. II. Cambridge, 1891.

TALMUD, the Jerusalem. Krotoschin, 1866.

------ the Babylonian. Frankfurt a. M., 1721.

TAWROGI (A. J.), Derech Erez Sutta. Königsberg, 1885.

TAYLOR (C.), Sayings of the Jewish Fathers, comprising Pirqe Aboth and Pereq R. Meir. Cambridge, 1877.

WOLFSOHN, see Ben Seeb.

YETSIRA (Sepher), see Lambert.

ZEDNER, Catalogue of Hebrew Books in the Library of the British Museum. (London), 1867.

ZOHAR, ed. Lublin, 1882.

ZUNZ (L.), Die gottesdienstlichen Vorträge der Juden ... zweite ... Auflage ... herausgegeben von Dr. N. Brüll. Frankfurt a. M., 1892.

BEN SIRA'S PROVERBS PRESERVED IN TALMUDIC AND RABBINIC LITERATURE.

I.
Sir. 3, 21.

a.

S^eadyah in ס" הגלוי *(ed. Harkavy), p. 178, 1. 18, quotes as an extract from the Wisdom of Eleazar ben Irai (see Preface) the following: (This seems to be the original text of Ben Sira.)*

Inquire not into that which is too difficult for thee;
    and that which is concealed from thee search not out.
Attend to that which is permitted to thee:
thou hast no business with hidden things.

b.
J. T. Ḥaghigah, II. (fol. 77^c).

That which is too difficult for thee, why shouldest thou know?
that which is deeper than Sheol, why shouldest thou search out?
Attend to that which is permitted to thee:
thou hast no business with hidden things.

c.
B. T. Ḥaghigah, fol. 130.

Inquire not into that which is too great for thee;
and that which is too hard for thee, search not out.
That which is too difficult for thee do not know;
and that which is concealed from thee do not ask.
Attend to that which is permitted to thee;
thou hast no business with hidden things.

II.
Sir. 4, 30. B. T. Gittin, fol. 6^b.

Let a man never bring excessive terror into his house.

III.
Sir. 5, 4. B. T. Haghigah, fol. 160.

If the evil propensity say to thee, Sin, for the Holy One (blessed be he!) excuseth, do not believe.

IV.
Sir. 5, 5.
S^{e}adyah, p. 176, 1. 19.

And be not confident of pardon,
to add iniquity to iniquity,
or say, His mercies are great,
he will pardon the multitude of my iniquities;
for mercy and wrath are with him,
and his might resteth upon the wicked.

V.
Sir. 5, 7. B. T. Shabbath, fol. 183ᵃ.

Repent one day before thy death.

VI.
Sir. 5, 15.

Great and small do not injure.

Aboth, IV. 6.

Despise not any man.

VII.
Sir. 6, 6. Sᵉadyah, op. cit., p. 178, l. 1; also B. T. Yebamoth, fol. 63ᵇ, and Synhedrin, fol. 100ᵇ, where the words of Micha 7, 5, follow.

Let those that are at peace with thee be many,
but reveal thy secret to one of a thousand
[keep the doors of thy mouth from her that lieth in thy bosom].

VIII.
Sir. 6, 7.
Sᵉadyah, p. 178, l. 3.

If thou gettest a friend, get him by proving,
and be not hasty to trust in him;
for there is a friend according to the occasion;
and he will not abide in the day of adversity.

IX.
Sir. 6, 13.
Sᵉadyah, p. 178, 1. 8.

Separate thyself from them that hate thee,
and be careful of thy friends.

X.
Sir. 7, 1. Cf. 12, 2.
Bereshith R., p. 44ª; Midrash Qoheleth v; Midrash Tanhuma חקת § 1.

Ben Sira said the proverb: Do not good to the evil, and evil will not befall thee.
See Schechter, *J. Q. R.* III. p. 694, No. 17 and note.

XI.
Sir. 7, 10.
B. T. Erubin, fol. 65ª.

Text has יורה 'to teach.' Rashi (Solomon of Troyes) says: I have searched to find this verse in the Hagiographa, but did not succeed. Perhaps it is in Sirach.
Rab said: Let not a man pray whose mind is not at rest within him, because it is said: In adversity who shall give thanks?
Perhaps a reminiscence of Ps. 6, 6.

XII.
Sir. 7, 17.
Aboth, IV. 7. Cf. No. LVI below.

Be humble exceedingly in spirit;
for the hope of man is a worm, and the son of man is a maggot (cf. Job 25, 6).

XIII.
Sir. 8, 5.
Mishnah Baba Metsia, IV. 10.

If a man repents, one does not say to him,
Remember thy former doings.

XIV.
Sir. 8, 8.
B. T. Sukkah, fol. 21^b, and Abodah Zarah, fol. 19^b.

Rab said: Even the ordinary conversation of the wise requires learning.

XV.
Sir. 8, 18.
B. T. Pesahim, fol. 49^b.

Six things are said of the people of the land (the unlearned) . . .; and they reveal not to him a secret.

XVI.
Sir. 9, 8.
B. T. Synhedrin, fol. 100^b; Yebamoth, fol. 63^b.
So Rashi (ap. Schechter, ibid., p. 100, note 36), ed.

Hide thine eyes from a comely woman,
lest thou be caught in her snares;
turn not aside to her, to mingle wine and strong drink with her:
for through the beauty of a fair woman many have been destroyed,
and 'all her slain are a mighty host' (Prov. 7, 26).

XVII.
Sir. 11, 1.

So in J. T. Berakhoth, vii. 2, and in Midrashim: the B. T. Berakhoth, fol. 48ᵃ, quotes Proverbs 4, 8, entire, omitting the last three words of the saying. See Reifmann's essay on Ben Sira in rpm III. p. 248, 3.

In the book of Ben Sira it is written:
Exalt her and she shall lift thee up (Prov. 4, 8), and set thee among princes.

XVIII.
Sir. 11, 8.
Aboth, V. 10.

Seven things are in a clod, and seven in a wise man. (The wise man) . . . does not interrupt the words of his companion; and is not hasty to reply . . .
Cf. Prov. 18, 13. Monatsschrift, 1865, p. 186, note 8.

XIX.
Sir. II, 9.
Midrash Tanḥuma (p. 73ᵃ) וארא, ה.

For he was busied with matters whereof he had no need.

XX.
Sir. 11, 28.
Seadyah, p. 178, 1. 6.

Call no one happy before (his) death,
for by his end shall a man be known.

XXI.
Sir. II, 29.
B. T. Synhedrin, fol. 100^b; Yebamoth, fol. 63^b.

Keep away many from the midst of thy house,
and bring not every man into thy house.

XXII.
Sir. 13, 2.
Aboth, II. 3.

Be cautious with (those in) authority,
for they let not a man approach them but for their own purposes;
and they appear like friends when it is to their advantage,
and stand not by a man in the hour of his need.
Monatsschrift, 1865, p. 186, note 8.

XXIII.
Sir. 13, 11^b.
S^{e}adyah, p. 578, 1. 15.

For with much talk will he try thee,
and will laugh at thee, and search thee out.
Cf. No. XXXIV below.

XXIV.
Sir. 13, 16.
B. T. Baba Qama, fol. 92b.

Thirdly, in the Hagiographa; as it is written:
Every bird dwelleth according to his kind,
and (so doth) man according to his like.

XXV.
Sir. 13, 25.
Ber. Rabba, fol. 64b.

The heart of a man changeth his countenance, whether for good or for evil.

XXVI.
Sir. 14, 5.
J. T. end of Peah.

Every one who needs to receive (alms) and refuses to take them, is (like) a shedder of blood, and it is forbidden to have compassion on him. If he has no pity on himself, how much less will he have pity on others?

XXVII.
Sir. 14 11.
B. T. Erubin, fol. 54

Rab said to his son Hamnuna:
My son, if thou hast aught, do good unto thyself,
for there is no pleasure in Sheol, and death tarries not.
And if thou sayest, It is for my sons and for my daughters,
who shall declare to thee the law in Sheol?
The sons of men are like the herbs of the field,
some flourish, and others fade.

XXVIII.
Sir. 16, 17.
S^{e}adyah, p. 178, l. 12.

Say not, I am hidden from God,
and in the height who shall remember me?
Among a numerous people I shall not be known,

or what is my soul among the multitude of spirits?

XXIX.
Cf. Sir. 18, 16, &c.
B. T. Baba Bathra, fol. 95.

He who gives a farthing to a poor man is blessed with six blessings, &c.:
but he who comforts him with words is blessed with eleven blessings.

XXX.
Sir. 18, 23.
Midrash Tanhuma § 8.

Ben Sira said:
Before thou vowest, make ready thy vows:
be not like a deceiver.

XXXI.
Sir. 20, 9.
Mishnah Berakhoth, IX. 3.

A man gives thanks for evil which results in good,
and for good which results in evil.

XXXII.
Sir. 20, 15.
J. T. Berakhoth, IV. 2.

Deliver not our livelihood into the hands of men (*lit.* flesh and blood),
for their giving is small, and their reproaching great.

XXXIII.
Sir. 21, 11.
B. T. Qiddushin, fol. 30^b.

I created the evil propensity:
I created against it the Law as a safeguard (*lit.* a seasoning).
If ye are occupied in the Law,
ye shall not be delivered into its hand.

XXXIV.
Sir. 21, 20.
Cf. also 19, 30.
B. T. Erubin, fol. 63b.

By three things a man is known, by his purse, by the wine-cup, and by his vexation. They say to him: By his laughter also.
Compare Aboth N., p. 86^a:
By three things do men test a man,
by trading (*lit.* giving and taking), and by much wine, and by much talking.

XXXV.
Cf. Sir. 21, 22. Also verse 23.
B. T. Niddah, 16^b.

Three things I hate, and four I do not love: (1) a prince who frequents the house of banqueting; (2) ....; (3) ....; (4) the man that enters suddenly the house of his neighbour.

XXXVI.
Sir. 21, 22.
פרקא דרבינו הקרוש ed. Schönblum; see Schechter, *J. Q. R.* III. p. 695, No. 21.

Let a man never hasten into the house of his neighbour; for thus it

is written in the book of Ben Sira:
>The foot of a senseless man hastens to (another's) house,
>but a prudent man will subdue many.

Let a man never look in at the door of his neighbour; for thus (it is written) in the book of Ben Sira:
>A foolish man gazes from the door into (another's) house,
>but a man's honour is in the house of his own kinsmen.

XXXVII.
Sir. 25, 2.
B. T. Pesahim, fol. 113b.

There are four things that the mind cannot bear.
They are these:
A poor man that is proud, a rich man that is a liar,
an old man that is an adulterer,
and a ruler that exalts himself above the multitude.
The last clause is not in Sirach.

XXXVIII.
Sir. 25, 3.
Aboth N., ch. 24 (p. 73).

Thus says the proverb:
If in thy youth thou hast had no delight in them,
how wilt thou attain them in thy old age?

XXXIX.
Sir. 25, 13.
B. T. Shabbath, fol. 11ª.

Rab said; Any sickness, but not sickness of the bowels;
any pain, but not the pain of the heart;
any ache, but not the aching of the head;
any evil, but not an evil woman.

XL.
Sir. 26, 1.
B. T. Yebamoth, fol. 63^b.

Happy is the husband of a beautiful woman:
the number of his days is doubled.

XLI.
Sir. 26, 3. B. T.
Synhedrin, fol. 100^b; cf. Yebamoth, fol. 63^b.

It is written in the book of Ben Sira:
    A good wife is a good gift;
    she shall be given into the bosom of him that feareth God.
    An evil wife is a plague (*lit.* a leprosy) to her husband.
    What is the remedy? Let him drive her from his house (i. e. divorce her),
    and he shall be healed from the plague of her (*lit.* from her leprosy).
    The second part not in Sirach.

XLII.
Sir. 28, 12.
M. Rabbah, Leviticus, fol. 153; and anonymously in Yalkut, Levit., § 460; Psalm, § 767; Job, § 501.

Bar Sira says:
There was a live coal before a man: he blew upon it and it flamed;
he spit upon it and it was extinguished.

XLIII.
Sir. 30, 23.
B. T. Yebamoth, fol. 63^b.

Be not troubled for the trouble of the morrow,
for 'thou knowest not what a day may bring forth' (Prov. 27, 1).
Perhaps on the morrow he will be no more,
and be found grieving over a world that is not his.

XLIV.
Sir. 30 (33), 33.
B. T. Baba Metsia, fol. 65ᵃ.

For it is better for him that his servant should not become an idler. So Rashi; cf. Kohut, *Aruch* s. v. סהר (II).

XLV.
Sir. 31 (34), 26.
Midrash Tanhuma (p. 26ᵇ) נח, ד.

Rabbi Johanan said: Any one who steals the worth of a farthing from his neighbour is as though he took away his life.

XLVI.
Sir. 31 (34), 27.
B. T. Baba Metsia, fol. 112ᵇ.

Every one who suppresses the hire of an hireling is as though he took from him his life.

XLVII.
Sir. 32 (35), 21.
Zohar, Levit. צו (3, p. 62).

That word mounts up, and cleaves the firmaments.

XLVIII.

Sir. 34 (31), 28.
Cf. the Syriac (31, 28).
B. T. Yoma, fol. 76ᵇ.

If he acts rightly, (i. e. drinks in moderation, Rashi,) it (wine) gladdens him; if he does not act rightly, (i. e. drinks to excess,) it ruins him.

XLIX.
Sir. 34 (31), 28. 29.
Zohar, Levit. שמיני, (3, p. 77).

But the beginning of wine is gladness, and the end thereof sorrow.

L.
Sir. 35 (32), 4.
B. T. Taanith, fol. 5ᵇ.

Men should not talk much at a meal.

LI.
Sir. 36 (33), 7.
B. T. Synhedrin, fol. 65ᵇ; Midrash Tanḥuma, Exodus תרומה, ג (p. 109ᵇ).

Turnus Rufus asked this question of R. Akiba, and said to him,
Why is one day different from another?
He said to him, And why is one man different from another?
He said to him, Because the Lord wills;
and the Sabbath also is because the Lord wills.

LII.
Cf. Sir. 36, 26.
B. T. Kethuboth, fol. 75ᵃ.

It is better to dwell two together, than to dwell a widow.

LIII.
Sir. 36, 30^b.
B. T. Shabbath, fol. 152^a.

The joy of the heart is a wife.
B. T. Yebamoth, fol. 62b.
Every man who has no wife, dwells without joy.

LIV.
Sir. 38, 1.
Midrash Rabba, Exodus, c. XXI.

(The proverb says); Honour thy physician before thou hast need of him.

The proverb also occurs in an Aramaic form: J. T. Taanith, III. 6.

In Midrash Tanhuma, Gen. מקץ, § 10 (p. 51^b), it is introduced with the words: אר׳ לעזר כתוב בספר בן סירא. See Schechter, *J. Q. R.* iii. p. 694, No. 16, and note 79.

I.V.
Sir. 38, 4.
Midr. Rabba, Genesis, viii; Midr. Yalkut, Job, § 501.

God causes spices to spring up out of the earth:
With them the physician heals the stroke,
and of them the perfumer compounds the perfume.

LVI.
Sir. 38, 24.
Aboth N., cap. 33, p. 73^b (cf. also Aboth, IV. 14).

Have little business, but be busied in the Law, and eager for the commandments;

and behave thyself in humbleness of spirit with every man.

LVII.
Sir. 39, 25.
Sepher Yetsira, p. 102, note 1.

Good is kept for the good,
and evil is kept for the evil.

LVIII.
Sir. 40, 19.
B. T. Berakhoth, fol. 57b.

Three things enlarge the understanding of a man. They are these:
a comely dwelling, a comely wife, and comely furniture.

LIX.
Sir. 40, 25.
B. T. Pesahim, fol. 119^a.

'And every (living) substance that followed them' (Dent. 11, 6, *lit.* that was at their feet). R. Eleazar says: This means the wealth of a man, which makes him stand firm upon his feet.

LX.
Sir. 40, 29.
B. T. Betsah, fol. 32^b.

There are three men whose life is no life. They are these:
The man who watches the table of his neighbour,
the man whose wife rules over him,
and the man whose body is ruled by pains.

LXI.
Sir. 42, 9.
B. T. Synhedrin, fol. 100^b.

A daughter is a vain treasure to her father:
for fear about her, he does not sleep;
in her youth, lest she be seduced;
in her maidenhood, lest she play the harlot;
when she is marriageable, lest she be not married;
when she is married, lest she have no sons;
when she is old, lest she practise sorcery.

LXII.
Sir. 9, 12 (Syriac).
Aboth, I. 5; Geiger in *ZDMG*. XII. p. 537.

And prolong not converse with a woman.

The following proverbs, ascribed to Ben Sira, are not found in the Greek or Syriac versions.

LXIII.
End of Derekh Erets Zuta (anonymous); Tanya, No. 10 (with the introductory words בן סירא אומר). See Schechter, *J. Q. R.* III. p. 695, No. 19.

The glory of God is the sons of men;
the glory of the sons of men is their clothing.

LXIV.
B. T. Baba Bathra, fol. 98^b; Yalqut Proverbs, § 956.

As it is written in the book of Ben Sira:
I have weighed all things in the balance,
and have found nothing lighter than bran;

but lighter than bran is the bridegroom who dwells in the house of his father-in-law,

and lighter than the bridegroom is a guest (*lit.* traveller) who introduces another guest,

and lighter than the guest is 'he that giveth answer before he heareth' (Prov. 18, 13).

LXV.
Baraitha Kallah, ed. Coronel, 7[b]. See Schechter, *J. Q. R.* iii. p. 697, No. 23.

It is written in the book of Ben Sira:
Remember the day of thy being gathered (in death);
withdraw (*lit.* gather in) reproach and acquire virtue (lit. merits);
for in the day of a man's being gathered, p. xxviii
neither riches nor great strength accompany him;
for his work is prepared, it will go before him,
and his righteousness shall lighten his eyes.

LXVI.
B. T. Synhedrin, fol. 100[b].

See marginal note to Sir. 40, 22, in the Hebrew text.

All the days of the poor are evil. Ben Sira says, the nights also. His roof is the lowest of roofs, and his vineyard is in the height of the mountains; the rain of other roofs falls on his roof, and the earth of his vineyard falls on other vineyards.

LXVII.
B. T. Synhedrin, 100[b].

As it is written: The thin-bearded is cunning and the thick-bearded is a fool.

This proverb is also found in the second Alphabet (see below).

LXVIII.

It is explained in the book of Ben Sira, that the Holy One (blessed be he!) is called 'place [1],' because he is the place of (i.e. contains) the world, and the world is not his place.

See Schechter (*J. Q. R.* III. p. 697, No. 24, and p. 706, note 109), who points out that the passage is probably taken from Bereshith Rabba (II), not from Ben Sira See No. I. *d*.

LXIX.
Baraitha Kallah, ed. Coronel, 7^b.

It is written in the book of Ben Sira; Love peace, for on it the world is stayed. Love all people, &c.

The rest of the passage is very corrupt, and cannot be translated without resorting to violent emendations. See Schechter, ibid., p. 696, and p. 705 for Reifmann's reconstruction.

The next two passages have been quoted as belonging to Ben Sira, but on insufficient grounds.

LXX.
B. T. Sota, 13^b; Bereshith R., § 19, beginning.

According to the camel, so is the burden.

LXXI.
J. T. Berakhoth, end.

In the scroll of the Ḥasidim it was found written:
For one day thou didst desert me,
and for two days will I desert thee.

LXXII.
The Alphabet of Ben Sira (*see above*).

אוקיר לאסיא עד דלא תצטריך ליה

Honour the physician before thou hast need of him.
Cf. above, No. LIV.

בר רלא בר שבקיה על אפי מיא וישט

The son who is not clear-witted, leave him upon the surface of the water and let him swim (trade).

גרמא רנפיל בתולקר בין טב או ביש גרדיה

The bone that has fallen to thy lot, whether it be good or evil, gnaw it.

דהבא צריך לקמצאה ועולימא להלקאה

Gold must be hammered, and a child must be beaten.

הוי טב וחולקיך מן טבתא לא תמנע

Be good, and thy portion of goodness do not refuse.

ווי ליה לבישא ווי להון לדבוקיהו

Woe to the wicked, and woe to them that consort with him.

זרוק לחמך על אפי מיא ואת משכח ליה בסוף יומיא

Cast thy bread upon the waters, for thou shalt find it at the end of the days.
Eccles. 11, 1.

חזית חמר אוכם לא אוכם ולא חיור

Hast thou seen white (l. חיור) and black (combined)? It (the result) is neither black nor white.

The readings are uncertain.

טב לביש לא תעביד ובישא לא ימטי לך

Do not good to the evil, and evil shall not befall thee.
Cf. above, No. X.

ידך מן טיבותא לא תמנע

Restrain not thy hand from doing good.
The Bodleian MS. (New Hebrew Catalogue, No. 1466) has ידך מן נגדא לעולמא לעולמא לא תמנע never restrain thy hand from chastising a child.

כלתא עלת לגנונא ולא ידעת מה מטי לה

The bride goes into the canopy, and knows not what is coming upon her.

לחכימא ברמיזא לשטיא בכורמיזא (חוטרא MS.)

For a wise man with a sign, for a fool with the fist.

מוקיר מבסרוהי דמה לחמרא

He who honours a man that despises him, is like an ass.

נור דליק מוקיד גדישין סגיאין

A fire when it is kindled (? l. קליל a little fire) burns many sheaves. Cf. Ep. of S. James 3, 5.

סבא בביתא סימנא טבא בביתא

An old man in a house is a good sign in the house.

ערבא טבא מאה צפרין ובישא אלף אלפין

A good surety is for a hundred days, but an evil surety is for a thousand thousand.

פתור פתורה פריש מחלוקת

Make clear the explanation, and remove differences.

צריך את למיסב ולמיתן יהא חולקך עם בר טבין

If thou must trade, let thy lot be with the lucky.

קריבא סחורתא אכלתיה מריה ורחיקא אכלא למרוה

Stock that is near at hand its owner consumes, but that which is far off consumes its owner.

רחימא קדמאה לית את כפר ביה

An old friend do not thou repudiate.

רחימך קדמאה לא תתכפר ביה ובעיקבא לית את נטר :MS. Bodl.
שיתין מליכין יהוון לך ומליכות נפשך לא תשבוק

Take sixty counsellors, but the counsel of thy heart do not abandon. Cf. above, No. VII.

תתיהב לן ידא כי הות שביעא ולא דהות כפינא

Let the hand be given to thee when it is satisfied, but not when it is hungry.
תתן לך ידא דהוה שביעא ולא דהוה בפיו ושבוע :MS. Bodl.

LXXIII.

With regard to the second Alphabet, see the Preface.

The first line (letter א) is similar to No. XLIII in our list of proverbs. Lines 2 (ב), 5 (ה), 16 (ע), 17 (פ) are from No. XVI in our list. Line 3 (ג) is from No. VII. Line 7 (ו?}) is from No. LXVII. Lines 9 (ט), 10 (י), and 11 (כ) from No. LXI.

The rest is not worth reprinting.

The Persian translation mentioned above (British Museum MS. Or. 4731) begins as follows:

בשם שדי בורא עולם באמירה. אתחיל לכתוב ספר בר סירא. אלפא
ביהא לבן סירא

כהיב עושה גדולות עד אין חוקר ונפלאות עד אין מספר. נוישתה אסת
כונאי בזורגי הא תא כה ניסת שמארי ועגאייב הא תא כה ניסת נהאייתי

(In Persian characters: نوشته است کونای بزورگیها تا
که نیست شماری وعجائبها تا که نیست نهایتی.)

The following sayings found in the work הפנינים, ascribed to Solomon ibn Gabirol (see above, p. xi), are cited by Reifmann (Haasyf, III. p. 250) as showing the influence of Sirach. The translation, which is from Ascher's edition, is rather free.

LXXIV.
Sir. 19, 10.

The sage was asked the surest means of keeping a secret. Said he, I make my heart its tomb.

LXXV.
Sir. 20, 18.
Ibid. 357.

He was wont to say, A slip of the tongue is more dangerous than the slip of the foot, for the slip of the tongue may cost thy head, whilst the slip of the foot may easily be cured.

LXXVI.
Sir. 20, 30 (and 41, 14).
Ibid. 58.

Wisdom lying dormant is like an unproductive treasure.

LXXVII.
Sir. 26, 28.
Ibid. 66, 67.

The sage observed, Pity the noble-hearted who has fallen; the rich that has become reduced; and the wise whose lot is cast amongst the fools. None deserves our pity more than the wise who has become subjected to the judgement of fools.

LXXVIII.
Sir. 30, 16.
Ibid. 457

There is no greater riches than health, no greater pleasure than a cheerful heart.

LXXIX.
Sir. 40, 28.
Ibid. 564.

Better the grave than a fall to poverty.

XXXIX. 15[c]

[With songs of the harp and of stringed instruments,

and thus with a shout shalt thou say;

16

All [the works of] God are good,

and he supplieth every need in its season.

17c

.... appraise ....

and the utterance of his mouth is his treasure.

18

In [his] place he maketh his pleasure to prosper,

and there is no restraint to his salvation.

19

The works of all flesh are before him,

and there is nothing hid from before his eyes.

20

He beholdeth from everlasting to everlasting:

[is there] limit to his salvation?

20ᶜ

There is nothing small or light with him,

and there is nothing too wonderful or hard for him.

21

None may say, Wherefore is this?

or all things are chosen for their uses.

21ᶜ

None may [say], This is worse than that,

for all things prevail in their season.

22

He maketh his blessings to overflow as the Nile,

and it saturateth the land like a river.

23

For his wrath dispossesseth nations,

and he turneth a watered land into salt.

24

[The path]s of the perfect man are plain,

so to strangers do they oppose themselves.

25

[Good things] he allotted to the [g]ood from the beginning,

so to the evil good and evil;

26

[The chief things] for the life of man are water,

and fire, and iron, and salt,

26ᶜ

[Flour of wheat], milk, and honey,

the blood of the grape, fresh oil, and clothing.

27

All th[ese] bring good to the [g]ood,

so for the evil they are turned to evil;

28

There be w[inds which are formed [for vengeance],

... [they] remove mountains.

29

Fire and hail, evil and pestilence,

these also are [formed] for judgement.

30

Beast of tooth, scorpion and cobra,

and a sword of vengeance to ban [the wicked].

30^c

All these are created for their uses,

and they are in his treasure-house, against the time when they are required.

31

When he commandeth them they rejoice,

and in their prescribed tasks they rebel not against his word.

32

Therefore from the beginning I took my stand, and I considered, and set it down in writing;

33

All the works of God are good;

he sufficeth for every need in its season.

34

None may say, This is evil, What is this?

for he maketh all things to prevail in their season.

35

Now with all (your) heart sing aloud,

and bless the name of the H[oly One].

XL. 1

Great occupation hath God allotted,

and a heavy yoke is upon the sons of men;

1c

From the day of his coming forth from his mother's womb,

until the day of his returning to the mother of all living;

3

From him that sitteth loftily on a throne,

even unto him that is clothed in dust and ashes.

4

From him that weareth a diadem and (priestly) plate,

even unto him that weareth a mantle [of poverty]:

5

Anger, jealousy, anxiety, and fear,

the terror of death, strife, and contention:

5ᶜ

And in the time when he resteth upon his bed,

the sleep of night changeth [his thoughts];

6

A little . . . . for a moment he is quiet,

and from the midst of terror[s he is perturbed?];

6ᶜ

. . . . . from the vision of his soul,

(he is) as a fugitive [hurrying on before] the pursuer.

9

. . . . [aw]aketh

... visions (?) ... rest.
[Pestile]nce and bloodshed, fever and drought,

devastation and destruction, evil and death.

10

Against the wicked, evil is created,

and because of him ruin departeth [not?].

11

All things that are from the earth return to the earth,

and that which is from the height (returneth) to the height.

13

Riches born of (?) riches are like an ever-flowing stream,

and as a mighty water-course in the flashing of thunder:

14

With his lifting up of (his) hands men rejoice,

for suddenly he perisheth for ever.

15

The branch of violence shall not be unpunished,

for the root of the godless is on the point of a crag.

16

Like axes (?) upon the bank of a stream,

before all rain they are extinguished.

17

But kindness shall never be moved,

and righteousness (*or* almsgiving) shall be established for ever.

18

A life of wine and strong drink is sweet,

but he that findeth a treasure is above them both.

19

A child and a city establish a name,

but he that findeth wisdom is above them both.

19^c

Offspring (of cattle) and planting make a name flourish,

but a woman beloved is above them both.

20

Wine and strong drink cause the heart to exult,

but the love of lovers is above them both.

21

Pipe and harp make sweet the song,

but a sincere tongue is above them both.

22

[Grace and beauty] delight the eye,

but the growing things of the field are above them both.

23

[A friend and a partner] behave [as occasion requires],

but a prudent wife is above them both.

24

A brother [and a helper are for a ti]me of adversity,

but righteousness (or almsgiving) delivereth above them both.

25

Gold and silver [make the foot stand sure]:

but [good counsels] is above them both.

26

Riches and strength lift up the heart,

but the fear of God is above them both.

26ᶜ

In the fear of the Lord there is no want,

and it needeth not to seek for [treasure] with it.

27

The fear of God is as an Eden of blessing,

and so all glory is its canopy.

28

My son, live not a life that subsists on giving:

better is he that is taken away (in death) than he that is importunate.

29

A man that looketh at the table of a stranger,

his life is not to be numbered as a life;

29c

His dainties are a loathing of the soul;

to a man that hath understanding (they are as) pains of the bowels.

30

Begging is sweet to the greedy man,

but in his inward parts it burneth as fire.

XLI. 1

Ah Death! how [bit]ter is the remembrance of thee

to a man that liveth qui[etly] in his place;

1c

To a man that is at ease and prospereth in all things,

and that hath yet strength to receive pleasure.

2

Aha Death! for acceptable (*lit.* good) is thy sentence

unto him that hath no might, and lacketh strength;

2c

(To) the man that stumbleth and striketh against all things, who loveth contradiction and hath lost hope.

3

Be not afraid of death (which is) thy sentence,

remember that they which went before and they which come after (will be) with thee.

4

This is the portion of all flesh from God,

and why dost thou refuse the law of the Most High?

4^c

Whether it be for a thousand years, or an hundred, or ten,

there are no corrections in Sh[eo]l.

5

A reprobate progeny is a byword of the evil,

and the offspring of the foolish is [. . . of the wic]ked.

6

From an unrighteous son cometh a rule of evil,

[and with his] seed [abideth want]

7

An ungodly father a [chi]l[d] doth curse,

because [on his] acc[ount he suffereth reproach].

8

[Woe] to [you, ye wicked,

because ye have forsaken the law of the Most] High.

9

If [ye increase, it shall be into] the hands of bodily mishap;

[and if ye] beget, it shall be for sighing.

If ye stumble, it shall be for perpetual joy;

9ᵇ

and if ye die, it shall be for a curse.

10

All things from nothing turn to nothing again,

so the godless (go) from emptiness to emptiness.

11

The vanity of man is in his body,

but a godly name shall not be cut off.

12

Fear for (thy) name, for that will accompany thee,

more than thousands of precious treasures.

13

The goodness of life hath days that may be numbered,

but goodness of name hath days without number.

14[b]

Buried wisdom and a hidden treasure,

what profit is in them both?

15

Better is a man that hideth his foolishness,

than a man that hideth his wisdom.

The discipline of shame.

14ᵃ

Hearken, O children, to the discipline of shame,

16

and be abashed according to my judgement.

16ᵇ

Not every kind of shame is it fitting to retain,

nor is every kind of abashment approved.

17

Be ashamed before father and mother, of whoredom;

before a prince sitting (in judgement), of a lie;

18

Before master and mistress of deceit;

before the congregation and the people, of transgression;

18ᶜ

[Before a partner] and a friend, of trespass;

19

and before the place where thou sojournest, of [a stranger;

19^b

[Of breaking an oath and a covenant,

of stretching out the elbow at meat;

19^d

Of refusing to grant a request;

21

of reckoning the face of thy friend;

21b

Of reckoning the dividing of a portion;

20

before him that saluteth, of silence;

20^b

Of gazing on a woman [that is a harlot?];

21^c

and of . . . . .

22ᶜ

Before a friend, of reproachful [word]s;

and after giving, spurn not.

XLII. 1

Of repeating a word that thou hearest,

and of laying bare any secret counsel:

1ᶜ

So shalt thou be truly shamefast,

and finding favour in the sight of all living.

1ᵉ

But of these things be not ashamed,

and accept not persons unto sin:

2

Of the law of the Most High and the statute,

and of judgement to do justice to the wicked,

3

Of reckoning with a partner and a master,

and of the division of an inheritance and a property,

4ª

Of the small dust of the scales and balance,

5ª

and of exchange by ephah and stone (weight),

4ᵇ

Of buying between much and little,

5ᶜ

and of smiting a deceitful [servant].

6

Upon an evil woman sets a seal,

but a place of weak hands thou mayest open.

7

In the place where thou committest a deposit, [count,

and let giving and receiving all be in writing.

8

(Be not ashamed) of the correction of the simple and the fool,

or of him that is grey-headed and very aged, and that (yet) taketh counsel for whoredom.

8ᶜ

So shalt thou be well-advised in truth,

and lowly before all living.

9

A daughter is to a father a deceptive treasure,

and the care of her [putteth away his sleep]:

9ᶜ

In her youth lest she commit adultery,

and in her virginity lest [she be defiled],

10

In her virginity lest she be seduced,

and in the house of [her lord lest she bear not?],

10ᶜ

In the house of her father lest [she play the harlot?],

and in the house of her hu[sband lest] . . . .

11

[My son, keep a strict watch over thy daughter,

lest she make thee] a name of evil odour,

11ᶜ

A byword in the city and a cursing of the people,

and shame thee [in the congregation of the gate.

11e

In the place where she lodgeth let there be no lattice,

nor a chamber looking upon the entrance round about.

12

Let her not show her beauty to any male,

and in the house of women let her not converse.

13

For from a garment cometh forth a moth,

and from a woman a woman's wickedness.

14

Better is the wickedness of a man than the goodness of a woman,

and the house of her that causeth shame poureth forth reproach.

15

I will remember now the works of God,

and that which I have seen I will recount.

15ᶜ

By the word of God is his pleasure,

and him that doeth his pleasure he hath accepted.

16

The rising sun is revealed over all things,

so the glory of the Lord is over all his works.

17

The saints of God do not suffice

to recount the wonders of the Lord'.

17ᶜ

God hath given strength unto his hosts,

that they may endure firmly before his glory.

18

He searcheth out the deep and the heart,

and understandeth all their nakednesses;

19

Declaring things that are past and that are to come,

and revealing the remotest of hidden things.

20

No knowledge is lacking to him,

and no matter escapeth him.

21

[The might of his wisdom] he hath regulated,

he is one from everlasting.

21c

Nothing [hath been added (unto him), or] diminished (from him),

and he hath no need of any instructor.

23a

He [establisheth all things for ever],

25ª

one thing upon another for the sake of its good.

25ᵇ

And who can [be filled with [beholding (his) beauty?]

XLIII. 1ª

. . . .

XLIII. 1ᵇ

And the body of heaven beholding his majesty,

XLII. 23ᵇ

and all things are obedient to every use.

24

All of them are different, one from another,

and he hath made none of them [in vain].

XLIII. 2

The sun, when he goeth forth, poureth out warmth:

how terrible are the works of the Lord!

3

By his shining he heateth the world;

before his drought who can maintain himself?

4

A fierce furnace is established by them (?),

the sun being sent forth setteth the mountains in a blaze.

4ᶜ

A tongue of light consumeth the inhabited(country),

and with its fire the eye is scorched;

5

For great is the Lord that made him,

and (with) his words he maketh brilliant (?) his mighty ones.

6

Moreover moon by moon the seasons return,

(for) a limited rule, but an everlasting sign;

7

By her are the appointed feast and the prescribed times,

and in her circuit [she doeth] (her) business;

8

With every (new) month she is renewed,

how terrible is she in her changing!

8^c

An instrument of the host of the (rain-)vessels on high,

paving the firmament with her shining:

9

The beauty of heaven, and the glory of a star,

and her light shining in the heights of God.

10

By the word of God a statute is established,

and they sleep not in their watches.

11

Behold the (rain)bow, and bless him that made it,

for exceeding majestic is it [in glory;

12

It compasseth with its glory the vault (of heaven),

and the hand of God hath stretched it out in [its pride].

13

His might marketh out the lightning,

and maketh brilliant the flashes [in judgement].

14

On that account he hath created a treasure-house,

and hath made [the clouds?] to fly forth . . . .

. . . .

. . . .

17

The voice of his thunder maketh his land to be in anguish,

the hot winds of the north, the tempest, and the whirlwind.

17c

Like darting flashes he sheddeth abroad his snow,

and like locusts (when) they settle is the falling down thereof;

18

The beauty of its whiteness dazzleth the eyes,

and the heart is disquieted at the raining of it.

19

The hoar-frost also he poureth out like salt,

and maketh it to bloom with flowers like sapphire.

20

The cold of the north wind he causeth to blow,

and congealeth his spring like rottenness (?).

20c

Over every standing water he spreadeth a crust,

and a pond putteth on as it were a breastplate.

21

It burneth up the produce like drought,

and the stateliness of growing things as a flame.

22

The dropping of a cloud healeth all things,

(even) dew releasing (?) the parched young grass.

23

His counsel burneth up (?) the great (deep),

and he planteth islands in the ocean.

24

They that go down to the sea tell of its bounds,

when we hear it with our ears, we are astonished.

25

Therein are wonders, the marvels of his work,

variety of all things living, and the mighty things of the great (deep).

26

By reason of him [his] messenger prospereth,

and by his words he performeth (his) pleasure.

27

More like this we will not add,

and the conclusion of the matter is, He is all.

28

Let us still be magnifying him, for we shall not search him out,

and he is great beyond all his works.

29

[The Lord is] exceeding [terrible],

and wonderful are his mighty acts.

30

[Ye that magnify the Lord], lift up your voice all that ye can, for there is yet more;

30ᶜ

ye that exalt him, renew your strength, and be not weary, for ye will not [search (him) out].

32

Many [hidden things hath he established (?) more than] these;

a little only have I seen of his works.

33

All things [hath the Lord made],

and to [the godly hath he given wisdom].

PRAISE OF THE PATRIARCHS.
XLIV. 1

Let me now praise godly men,

our fathers in their generations.

2

Great glory the Most High allotted (to them),

and they were great from days of old;

3

Rulers of the earth in their royalty,

and men of renown in their might;

3ᶜ

Who gave counsel by their understanding,

and saw all things in their prophecy;

4

Princes of nations in their prudence,

and potentates in their care;

4ᶜ

Wise of meditation in their writing,

and governing in their watchfulness;

5

Who sought out music according to rule,

and took up the proverb in writing;

6

Men of worth, and supported with strength,

and that lived quietly upon their places.

7

All these in their generation (were honoured),

and from their birth was their glory.

8

There be of them that have left a name,

that men might tell of it in their inheritance;

9

And there be of them which have no memorial,

and have ceased as they have ceased;

9c

They were as though they had not been,

and their children after them.

10

Nevertheless these were godly men,

and their hope [shall not perish;

11

With their seed their goodness remaineth sure,

and their inheritance unto chil[dren's children];

13

Their memory standeth fast for ever,

and their righteousness [shall not be forgotten];

14

[Their bodies were buried in p]eac[e,

but their name liveth] unto all generations a.

16

Enoch [was f]ound perfect, and walked with the Lord, and was taken,

being an example (*lit.* sign) of knowledge to all generations.

17

Noah the righteous was found perfect,

in a season of destruction he became the successor;

17ᶜ

For his sake was there a remnant,

and through the covenant with him, the flood ceased;

18

By an everlasting sign was it made with him,

that he would not destroy all flesh.

19

Abraham was the father of a multitude of nations,

he put no blemish upon his glory;

20

Who kept the commandment of the Most High,

and entered into a covenant with him;

20^c

In his flesh he made him an ordinance,

and when he was proved he was found faithful.

21

Therefore he promised him with an oath,

that he would bless the nations in his seed,

21^e

To cause them to inherit [from se]a to sea,

and from the River unto the ends of the earth.

22

To Isaac also did he raise up a son,

for the sake of Abraham his father;

22^c

He gave him (?)the covenant of every ancestor,

23

and the blessing rested on the head of Israel;

23^b

And he confirmed him in the blessing,

and gave him his inheritance;

23^d

And he set him in tribes,

in twelve parts.

23^f

[And he brought ou]t of him a man,

who found favour in the sight of all living,

XLV. 1

[A man beloved of] God and men,

(even) Moses, whose memory is unto good'.

2

[And G]od 9 glorified him

and strengthened him in the heights (of heaven).

3

By [his words] . . . .,

and gave him boldness before the king;

3c

And gave him a charge unto [his people],

and sh[ewed him of his glory].

4

For his faithfulness and meekness,

he chose him out of all [flesh];

5

And made him to hear his voice,

and caused him to draw near into the thick darkness;

5ᶜ

And set a commandment in his hand,

even the law of life and understanding;

5ᵉ

To teach in Jacob his statutes,

and his testimonies and judgements unto Israel.

6

And he exalted a holy man, even Aaron of the tribe of Levi,

7

and set him for an everlasting ordinance;

7ᵇ

And put majesty upon him,

and he ministered unto him in his glory.

7ᵈ

And he girded him about (as) with the towering horns of a wild-ox,

and clothed him with bells.

8

And he clothed him with the perfection of adornment,

and adorned him with glory and strength;

8ᶜ

The breeches, the coats, and the robe,

9

and [compassed him] with bells,

9ᵇ

And pomegranates, a multitude round about,

to make music with his steps;

9ᵈ

To make the sound of him to be heard in the inmost temple,

for a memorial to the children of his people.

10

Holy garments, of gold, blue, and purple,

the work of the designer:

10ᶜ

The breastplate of judgement, the ephod, and the waist-cloth,

11

and scarlet, the work of the weaver;

11ᵇ

Pleasant stones upon the breast-plate,

the engravings of a signet with settings;

11ᵈ

Every precious stone for a memorial with graven writing,

according to the number of [the tribes of Israel;

12

The crown of pure gold, the robe, and the mitre,

and the plate, [having engraven on it, as on a signet,] Holiness;

12ᶜ

Majesty, glory, and the praise of strength,

the desire [of the eyes, and the perfection of b]eauty.

13

Be[fore them were no]t [any such,

and no] stranger [should put them on for ever].

13ᶜ

He [trusted him and] his sons after this manner,

and thus (should) his sons (do) throughout their generations;

14

His meal-offering should be wholly burnt,

and every day twice continually.

15

And Moses filled his hand,

and anointed him with the holy oil.

15ᶜ

And it was unto him an everlasting covenant,

and to his seed as the days of heaven,

15ᵉ

To minister and to execute the priest's office unto him,

and to bless his people in his name.

16

And he chose him out of all living,

to bring near the burnt-offering and the fat pieces;

16ᶜ

And to burn a sweet savour and a memorial,

and to make atonement for the children of Israel.

17

And he gave him his commandments,

and made him to have authority over statute and judgement.

17ᶜ

So he taught his people statutes,

and judgements unto the children of Israel.

18

But strangers were incensed against him,

and were jealous of him in the wilderness;

18e

The men of Dathan and Abiram,

and the congregation of Korah in the violence of their anger.

19

And the Lord saw it and was angered,

and consumed them in the heat of his anger;

19c

And he brought upon them a sign,

and devoured them with his flaming fire.

20

And [he increased] to Aaron his glory,

and gave him his inheritance;

20e

The holy f[irst-fruits] he gave to him for bread,

21a

that they should eat the fire-offerings of the Lord;

20ᵈ

.... they should divide,

21ᵇ

and (they should be) a gift to him and to his seed;

22

Only [in the land of his people] he should not inherit,

and amongst them he should not divide an inheritance;

22ᵉ

The fire-offerings of the Lord [should be their portion and their inheritance]

.... Israel.

23

Moreover Phinehas, the son of Eleazar,

in might .....

23ᶜ

In his jealousy for the God of all,

and stood in the breach of his people.

23ᵉ

Whose heart made him willing,

and he made atonement for the children of Israel.

24

Therefore for him also did he establish an ordinance,

a covenant of peace to maintain the sanctuary;

24ᶜ

Which should be to him and to his seed,

an high priesthood for ever.

25

Also his covenant (was) with David

the son of Jesse, of the tribe of Judah.

25ᵃ

An inheritance of fire in presence of his glory

was the inheritance of Aaron unto all his seed.

25ᵉ

And now bless ye the Lord, the good,

who hath crowned you with glory;

26

And given you wisdom of heart,

26^c

that your goodness [and] your [mig]ht be not forgotten through perpetual generations.

XLVI. 1

A mighty man of valour was Joshua the son of Nun,

the minister of Moses in prophecy,

1^c

Who was formed that there might be in his days

a great salvation to his chosen ones;

1^e

To execute vengeance upon the enemy,

and to give Israel his inheritance.

2

How glorious was he when he stretched out his hand,

when he swung the javelin against the city!

3

Who was he that could stand before him?

for he fought] the battles of the Lord.

4

Did not the sun stand still by his hand,

so that one day [became two]?

5

For he called unto God Most High,

when he was pressed upon [round about].

5c

And God Most High answered him with stones

of [hail and coa]ls [of fir]e;

6

. . . .

and in [the descent]

6ᶜ

That every banned nation [might kn]ow

that the Lord watched their battles.

6ᵉ

[Yea], because he followed fully after God,

7

and in the days of Moses wrought godliness,

7ᵇ

[H]e, and Caleb the son of Jephunneh,

in standing fast when the assembly cast off restraint,

7ᵈ

To turn away wrath from the congregation,

and to still the evil report;

8

Therefore they also, two alone, were reserved,

out of six hundred thousand men on foot,

8ᵉ

To bring them into their inheritance,

a land flowing with milk and honey.

9

And he gave strength unto Caleb,

and even unto old age it remained with him;

9ᶜ

To make him to tread upon the high places of the land,

and that his seed also should possess an inheritance;

10

That all the seed of Jacob might know

that it was good to follow fully after the Lord.

11

Also the judges every one by his name,

every one whose heart had not turned aside,

11ᶜ

And who drew not back from (following) after God--

may their memory be blessed, 12^b and their name succeed to their sons.

13

The lover of his people, & acceptable to his Maker,

(was) he who was lent from his mother's womb,

13^c

A nazirite of the Lord in prophecy,

Samuel, who was judge and priest.

13^e

[The pro]phet of God established a kingdom,

and anointed leaders' over the people.

14

By [his law he commanded the congregation,

and the God of Jacob visited (them).

15

By . . . . he was [san]ctified a gazer (prophet),

and by his word also he was confirmed as a shepherd.

16

He also [called] unto God,

[when] his [ene]mies [pressed hi]m round about,

16ᶜ

When he offered up [a sucking lamb,

17

and [the Lord] thun[dered out of heaven];

17ᵇ

With a mighty crash his voice was heard,

18

and he subdued the garrisons of the foe, and des[troy]ed all the lords of the Philistines.

19

And at the time of his resting upon his (last) bed, he called the Lord and his anointed to witness, (saying,)

19ᶜ

From [whom] have I [taken] a ransom or a secret gift? and no man answered against him.

19ᵉ

Also till the time of his end he was found prudent in the sight of the Lord and in the sight of all living.

20

And even after his death he was sought, and declared to the king his ways, 20ᶜ and lifted up his voice from the earth in prophecy.

XLVII. 1

Moreover after him rose up Nathan,

to stand before David.

2

For like fat separated from the holy (offering),

so was David (separated) from Israel.

3

He mocked at lions as at a kid,

and at bears as at the herds of Bastian.

4

In his youth he smote a mighty man,

and took away an everlasting [reproach],

4c

When he swung his hand upon the sling,

and brake the pr[id]e of Goliath.

5

For he called unto God Most High,

and he put strength in his right hand,

5c

To thrust away the man skilled in battles,

and to exalt the horn of his people.

6

Therefore the daughters sang of him,

and titled him with ten thousand.

6c

When he had put on the diadem he fought,

7

and subdued the adversary round about;

7ᵇ

And set nakedness among the Philistines,

and brake [their h]orn in pieces unto this day.

8

In all his works he gave thanks to God

Most High [with words of glory,

8ᶜ

With his whole heart loving him that made him,

and every [day] . . . .

9

Stringed instruments of song (he sets) be[fore the altar],

and the sound of [. . . . and of harps he set in order.

10

. . . .

. . . . [year by y]ear.

10ᶜ

While [they praised his holy name,

the sanctuary resounded before the morning.

11

.... the Lord took away his transgression,

and exalted his horn for ever,

11ᶜ

[And ga]ve him the ordinance of the kingdom,

and established his throne over Jerusalem.

12

[And] among the people there arose none after him,

an understanding son, dwelling securely.

13

Solomon reigned in days of prosperity,

and God gave rest to him round about,

13ᶜ

Who established an house for his name,

and set up a sanctuary for ever.

14

How wast thou wise in thy youth!

and didst make instruction to overflow like the Nile:

15

The earth . . . .

and thou didst celebrate song in the height (?);

16

With songs, proverbs, dark sayings, and figures,

thou didst greatly move the nations:

17

Thou wast called by the glorious name,

which is called over Israel,

18ᶜ

And thou didst heap up gold as iron,

and didst multiply silver like lead;

19

But thou gavest thy loins unto women,

and lettest them have dominion over thy body;

20

So [thou] didst put a blemish upon thy glory,

and didst profane thy couch,

20ᶜ

[To bring] wrath upon thy issue,

and sighing upon thy bed;

21

That [they should become] two tribes,

and that out or Ephraim a kingdom of violence (might arise).

22

[Nevertheless] God forsaketh not mercy,

nor letteth any of his words fall to the ground.

22ᶜ

He will not [cut off from his chosen] progeny and offspring,

nor destroy them that [lo]ve him;

22^e

So he gave unto [Jacob a remnant],

and to [David] . . . .

23

And Solomon slept. . . . .

and left of his [seed] af[ter him].

23^c

Ample in foolishness and lacking understanding,

Rehoboam by [his counsel let loose [the people;

23^e

Until there arose--let him have no memorial!--Jeroboam, the son of Nebat, who made [Israel to si]n.

23^g

And he gave unto Ephraim a stumbling-block,

24^b

to drive them out [of] their land.

24ᵃ

And his sin was great exceedingly,

25

and he sold himself to all evil.

XLVIII. 1

Till there arose a prophet like fire,

whose words were like a burning furnace.

2

And he brake for them the staff of bread,

and by his jealousy made them few in number.

3

By the word of God he shut up the heavens,

. . . . fires.

4

How terrible wast thou, O Elijah!

he who is like thee may glory!

5

Who didst raise up one that expired from death,

and from Sheol, according to the will of the Lord;

6

Who broughtest down kings to the pit,

and honourable men [from] their beds;

7

Who anointedst one filled with retribution,

and a prophet to succeed in thy place;

8

Who heardest reproofs in Sinai,

and judgements of vengeance in Horeb;

9

Who wast taken up by a whirlwind on high,

and by troops of fire [into heaven];

10

Who art written down as ready for a season,

to snake anger to cease before . . . . . .

10ᶜ

To turn the heart of the fathers to the children,

and to give understanding to the tr[ibes of Isra]el.

11

Happy he that saw thee and died (?) . . . .

. . . . .

12

Elijah. . . . .

and Elisha . . . .

12ᶜ

With a do[uble] measures he multiplied signs,

and he was learned in every utterance of his mouth.

12ᵉ

All his life long he quaked before none,

and no flesh had dominion over his spirit;

13

No matter was too hard for him,

and from its place his flesh prophesied;

14

In his life he did wonders,

and in his death marvellous works.

15

For all this the people turned not,

and ceased not from their sins,

15^c

Till they were rooted up from their land,

and were scattered through all the earth.

15^e

But there were left to Judah a few,

and still a judge to the house of David.

16

There were of them that dealt uprightly,

and there were of them that trespassed wondrously.

17

Hezekiah strengthened his city,

when he turned aside waters into the midst of it,

17ᶜ

And hewed the rocks with brass,

and stopped up mountains for a pool.

18

In his days came up Sennacherib,

and sent Rabshakeh;

18ᶜ

And he stretched out his hand against Sion,

and blasphemed God in his pride.

19

[Then were] they melted in the pride of their heart,

and were in anguish as a woman in travail;

20

So they called] unto God Most High,

and spread forth their hands unto him;

20ᶜ

And he [heard] the voice of their prayer,

and saved them by the hand of Isaiah;

21

And [he smote the c]amp of the Assyrian,

and discomfited them with the plague.

22

[For Hezekiah [did] that which was go[od,

and] was strong in the ways of David.

24

By a spirit of might he saw the end,

and comforted the mourners of Sion.

25

For ever he declared things that should be,

and hidden things before they came.

XLIX. 1

The name of Josiah is like incense of sweet spices,

salted, the work of the perfumer;

1^c

His memory is sweet as honey on the palate,

and as music at the banquet of wine.

2

For he was grieved for our backslidings,

and he made the abominations of vanity to cease;

3

And he made his heart perfect toward God,

and in days of violence he wrought godliness.

4

Except David, Hezekiah, and Josiah,

they all did corruptly;

4e

And forsook the law of the Most High,

the kings of Judah, till they were ended.

5

So he turned their horn backward,

and (gave) their glory to a foolish, foreign nation;

6

And they set on fire the holy city,

and made her ways desolate.

6e

By the hand of Jeremiah, for they afflicted him,

yet from the womb he was formed (to be) a prophet,

7c

To pluck up and to break down and to destroy (and) to overthrow,

and in like manner to build up, to plant, and to make strong.

8

Ezekiel saw the vision,

and declared divers kinds of chariot.

9

Also he made mention of Job,

who maintained all the w[ays of righ]teousness.

10

Moreover the twelve prophets,

may their strength flou[rish out of their pla]ces.

10ᶜ

Who recovered Jacob to health,

and restored him by . . . .

11

[How shall we magni]fy [Zerubbabel]?

. . . .

---

1. A common Rabbinical designation of God. Cf. τόπος in Philo (e. g. de Somniis, I. § 11, ed. Mangey, I. 630).

Copyright © 2019 / Alicia Éditions
Credits: Canva, introduction to Sirach, codex sinaiticus
All rights reserved